Gallery Books
Editor Peter Fallon

THE GRAVITY WAVE

Peter Sirr

THE GRAVITY WAVE

Gallery Books

The Gravity Wave
is first published
simultaneously in paperback
and in a clothbound edition
on 15 August 2019.

The Gallery Press
Loughcrew
Oldcastle
County Meath
Ireland

www.gallerypress.com

ISBN 978 1 85235 765 2 *paperback*
       978 1 85235 766 9 *clothbound*

A CIP catalogue record for this book
is available from the British Library.

The Gravity Wave receives financial assistance
from the Arts Council.

Contents

for Enda and Freya
and in memory of my mother

The Now Slice

Breakfast is over, you've gone to the hard world.
Ulysses struggles from a speaker, nearly dead.
He flails in the waves, a towering headland
staring him down. Where's help here?
The floor turns stone, the kitchen Mycenaean.
The dog sprawls on the couch, lost in a dream
of toast and cats. A fruit fly climbs a jar
to dangerous honey. I lift my cup and a star
explodes, a meteor crashes into the moon.
A blue alien looks out along his slice of time.
He's going to school, maybe. When he comes back
the future will already be over. Only Ulysses
will still be here. He's found a riverbank now
and friendly leaves. Athena rains down sleep on his eyes.

Home

Diminished? Really? Gods don't hold us, the temples
wither, the priests are all in sales
but the sun still shines, the oxen low
and the winedark sea is still as dark as wine.

Come with me now to where dawn
dips her rosy toes by the harbour wall.
Lust for home is overrated, it's the lust
for time that kills us all. This place was lost

when you first looked back, the only home
is the air you stand in, your creaking bones.
Creak on. Live in the changes, the builders' dust,
the harbour light, this

wary kiss   or calypso back to heartbreak
hammock, unaltering day, everlasting night.

Operatic

Everywhere difficulty, everywhere
the resourceful fury of gods and men,
our own monstrous angers. Impossible to come back.
We sit in the dark, oceans between us.

If only we were *there*, beyond the lutes and the cellos,
singing our way home. If we could walk out
to a light like this, magicked to the centre
of what it all comes down to, the sudden

astonishing burst, the twenty-four bars where Neptune relents
and the dead suitors walk on stage bearing candles.
Let him live! The chorus is on fire, *is* fire,

and surely nothing can be difficult now, surely now
we can climb out of the waves at last,
into a hard, enduring music of return.

Blackbird

There was so much to do at the end.
Possessed with what must outlive you
you flailed from corner to corner of a white room,
then slumped over a laptop, mind
on fire, the unstoppable present
flooding your fingertips. How much time
to harvest a self . . . words sprawled across the screen,
words like nails hammered to a sinking board

until the blackbird sang outside
and the world swung open to that one tune.
The blackbird floods the morning, floods the bone.
The blackbird owns the air, blackbird
sings *tomorrow, tomorrow, tomorrow*
to the fading laptop, the empty room.

Radio Life

This was your radio, all the days you sent me.
Your voice from the woods, the kitchen table.
I slip the cassette into the player
like the curator
of a museum of obsolescence.

We're in there, obsolescing, the tapes frayed.
We might be Hittites. And yet
let the technologies rot. The air holds us
and no one comes to see it, no one
interrogates it. You sit down

somewhere again, in a dark studio.
Silence, the trees signing outside.
A light flares, your voice comes on
as if a great switch has been thrown.

Deer, Phoenix Park

How many are there? I glance like an actor
counting the audience.
Are we the set they're looking at?
We don't seem to have entered yet
or they don't see us. The road
is beyond them. I slow the car.
I don't want to count deer, I want
to count *in* deer. Antler, Forest, Eyes,
Stillness, Speed, Hide . . . I'd like
this currency to fall between us
where we step invisibly from the car
slipped from ourselves to kneel
grass-lit and concentrated, close to a road
that keeps wobbling and clarifying
like the rim of the world or the end of speech.

Robotics

The fake poets come up on the fake news.
Robot lyrics cram the playlists, ice
assembles in the fist. Help love in winter
it is not as in the summer the language
is somehow different, a cold flows through us.
All these lies make an algorithm of the heart.
Wanly it beats. Jack Keats, Jake Eats, Eddie
Rocket's tasteful sonnets. A fake snow
blows from the page. The clouds are real, the larks
have their own channel. Up they go. Autumn, listen,
falls through the earbuds. The studio is bursting
with startup stanzas, this one has reached its target,
it's on its way to a soul near you. Love's
broken, a coaltruck clattering, blackening your street.

Naming the Street

for Freya

You say the name and the buildings sharpen,
the late morning light touching the brick
as if belatedly or as if the street moved back
a fraction from my sight and said,
'It's hers now, her step we wait for, her eyes
the houses move towards. The place is printed
on her glance first. After that, we move for you
as, I don't know, a shopkeeper mops his brow
and turns to a less favoured customer. What is it?
What did you think, the city lay pressed to your face,
lifting its veils, opening all its doors and gates?
The parks are full, a thousand autumns cross the bridge.
Wherever you think you're walking is farther back, a dim
retreat. But look up now and listen to her say our name . . .'

Add to Dictionary

Shahad, Rawan, Maram
this hand in the rubble
these broken shutters
shrapnel on the bed cover
ignore all
you possibly can but come back
to this, Abu Omar in his shattered room
listening to the last music in the world
on his wind-up record player

Add to strategy
the barrel bombs on the hospital
the mourners buried at the funeral
ignore all, in sleep return
add to shelter
the child in the underground nursery
crying *Joy, that's what I love*
add peril
unignorable, add to dictionary
al-Kalleseh, al-Firdous, al-Salheen

Add to debris
this wrecked souk, this
persistent bread,
add to city
every broken street, smashed courtyard
ignore
nothing, let the pages
spread their maps
till every bone is pinned,
every lost breath uttered

News from the Old World

A little further up, where Misery Hill
turns towards Deadman's Pond,
past the old battery, cannons trained
on the ghosts of submariners
snagged on chains slung across the narrows

pausing to feast your eyes
then keeping the gibbet to your left
and following the path to the summit
where the wind arrives like an old score
past the stocks, the whipping post

coming eventually to the signal tower
where the first message bridged
distance unimaginable
from a hill like this to carry
all the news that could be caught

songs of weather and time
grass smells, sheep's breath, wrist
to shackled wrist, a hood pulled down
over a mumbled prayer
the drums' remorseless code . . .

Eurydice Awake

I kept
my visor down, waiting
like a courier in the lobby
for someone to come. No one came,
there were no instructions,
no guides or plans, no signals
crackling in the headset.
Where were you? But then
it came to me, the wreckage
spilled out all over the hillside,
the mitigating, falsifying acres
as if the whole country had killed you
or none of it, or nothing claimed it —
threads of a tunic, bloodstained clods,
hair and nails, a broken plectrum,
the body parts, the mutilations
when they showed,
like videos calmly posted —
it was all
forensics and after-quiet
and I gathered what I could
crouched in the dusk
singing softly to the hillside
and carried the bag back down.
No one looked or queried. The transports
were full and everyone tuned
to their own devices.
I sit now in the lounge
reading the report and playing back
the old music and you come
prancing through the headphones,
swinging the mike from hand to hand
as if it were all still waiting,
the stadium full and the lighters flaring,
everything plugged in, tested,

ready to explode,
and I had stood behind you, arms stretched out,
your body retreating to my breath,
your shirt falling on my eyes
as you yell redemption
and strike the opening chord.

❖

And if you hadn't turned,
what then?
What would have followed you out?
Look, home again,
head to the lamp-spill,
retrieving and retrieving . . .
and there am I, bone-empty,
watching you hunched over the desk
till dawn shreds the book, blanks the screen
and you turn to me again the dark unseeing
obols of your eyes.

❖

Climb the sloping path through the pines,
your eager feet on the stones,
there's a sudden sharpness in your breath,
your eyes looking back to where
the city spreads across the plain,
to a sun-softened headland . . .
look out, look up, look back,
your eyes, your hands,
the rustle in the hedgerow,
the song in the branches
are mine,

the paused air where you stand
in the middle of the car park,
the door opening, the car reversing,
the hands on the wheel are mine,
the gears shift under my palm,
traffic pulses under my skin,
Cerberus paws the soles of your feet,
I step from you,
then turn and take you in my arms
where you creak and crumble and almost dissolve,
cat got your tongue,
mouse got your eyes,
till you look at me, look at me, look at me,
the dogs roll back the stone
and the flesh grows back on the bone.

❖

From the ruin of the riverbank,
from the dogs and the desks and the corridors
ravaged, torn, pawed at and gaped at,
charming no one, no sweet smiles
or persuasive repertoire
and for no greater purpose
than to sit on the grass in the sun and the rain
or walk through the streets at dawn,
following no one and wanting nothing
but the place waking to itself
before I go back down.

'Say goodbye, Catullus...'

Triptych by Cy Twombly, 1928-2011, Menil Museum, Houston

Say goodbye, Catullus, to the shores of Asia Minor,
these hungry streets don't know your tread.
City piles on city, deepening red
where evening streams down the avenues
and the fountains pillars vendors huddle.
It's spring again and the great friends have returned
to the boiling pots they came from,
the days have gone back, the pulsing skin.
Plectrums fall from the sky, a world all fingers
plucks and sings.

Beautiful brothers for whom
through border after border we struggled,
you're ashes now and will not listen.
Say goodbye to trembling yellow and bursting black,
suns of red and orange flaming down
to poor remembered boats, colours
seeking their own erasure. The sea will wind you back
from hand to hand, lover to waiting lover,
all the way to the smudge at the end of the canvas,
end or beginning, now or forever,
ave breathing in the mouth of *vale*.

'Some say . . . '

Homage to Sappho

Some say a fleet of ships
some streets in May

some say blood some wine
a summer sky some say

hawk in flight some oak
entrenched   but I

I think of you   leave
the torn world to brood

and stew   if Helen
can do it so can I without

turning without
a thought or turning back

forget ships horses muscled
soldiery   there's this

there's you
swooping from the air

pinioned to the ground
my own hawk tree

quick ship gliding
to its shimmering coast

❖

Some say moor grass, marigold
some a kestrel hovering

above the marshland
some say silk some snow

dusting the city pavement
the green chill

of winter meadows   but I
I say it's cold outside

these landscapes will return
it's the room that havers   the bed

that will abandon us
some say run some stay

but I   I think of your hands
combing the grasses

your lips fly your heart
pulses   dithers

some say earth some sky
some hesitate some fly

but I   but I

'We move lightly . . .'

We move lightly
almost as if
we weren't here,
as if nothing
could see us, hear us;

through forests, cities,
in the gleam of the river;
or we'd become
feather drift, water
whisper, wind curving

in the cooling sun;
moving to leave
earth unstepped on, air
unpushed through, where
smallness abounds, dust

feasts, we moved feasting
through the grasses,
as though this were us,
the heron's wings above the water,
the heron's stillness

under the branches; every
small gesture, what's missed
or hardly here, moving
on a long path already
forgotten; this tree

arching its slender body
across the stream
where we might touch
both root and tip,
fording desire, and keep

going, first
word, last breath,
registering everything, moving
always and forever
but lightly, disturbing nothing.

Blue Octavo: Images from Kafka

Written while listening to Max Richter's The Blue Notebooks

I THE ROOM

There's a room inside us we've never settled,
never owned.
To get there is to find the movers
have just filled their van
and driven off.

Yet constantly they return,
their hands weighed down,
the floor rising to meet them again.
The windows are closed,
the windows are open.

Everything you see is here to stay,
sliding quietly away.
To walk around in the early hours
is to hear
deep inside

the rocking of the furniture,
the grief of the floor,
in the quietest hour of all.
The mirror
loosening on the wall.

2 THE TREES

The night after I heard
they'd long since bulldozed
the house where I was born,
that not a thing survived,

that even the name had gone
and the garden was destroyed
that sloped gently to the river

I fell asleep and dreamed
that I went back there
my wings outstretched
above the sunlit brick
and the heart-bursting
infinite garden.

I saw that the trees
were higher than they'd ever been,
that in all the years
since they'd been cut down
they'd kept on growing.
I woke to find
the leaves still scattered in my room.

Signals

Despatched by curious worlds
all around us the signals wait

shadows, legates, heralds
greeting, probing

we're here
or were, and are dust now

our suns burnt out
our songs vaporized

whole civiliszations
under our fingers, between our toes

turning with us
in the depths of the night

for all we know
on our tiny dot

for everything we understand
an equal unknowable

for every sign an unreceivable
countersign

for every prayer a counterprayer
under a cup, a mouth

between
the doorjamb and the door

for every breath a counterbreath
All our lovely

counterlives!
Lean

on us, let us in, send
something we might imagine

but won't decode
to accompany us

in the great darkness

Ode

Into your memory
I consign, again,
aubergines, spices,

teaspoons, tablespoons,
thimblefuls,
hints and suspicions,

secrecies
and improvisations.
Hunched and edgy,

I twist and turn,
pour this and that,
while you sit back, relax,

remember
your childhood in France,
your dreams of better use.

You'll live forever:
already
the nose of the future

hovers above you,
you're in good hands,
better than mine,

my daughter's daughter's
long lost twin
come back

to heat you long,
dribble oil and onion
and let the spices rip.

But before the doorbell rings
and the hungry coats
come in, before

the knives, the forks,
the curious glances
into your depths,

remember this,
keep a little of our own
peculiar dance,

just the two of us
alone in the gloom
riffing, whispering

as, who knows where,
another city,
a Martian dusk,

hunched, edgy,
shaking this and that
she tests and pours,

sinks one thing
after another into your
forgiving embrace

then stops,
suddenly, in her
interplanetary kitchen,

the spoon in her mouth,
an ancient history
salting her tongue.

The Street

The street sign is there, but where's the street?
Missing, the guidebook says, an oversight,
the namers dozing on their ladders,
a prankster in the foundry. But we know differently
who live in the city, though we can't be sure.
The elders were offended, the place insulted.
Exiled, banished, bored, it packed its bags,
bought its ticket for another life.
Troubled Alley, Had Enough Lane —
we won't ever see your like again.
You're parked on a cloud, with all your wares,
still open for business; you whisper to shadows
in a new language by an old canal
or you've snuck back underground to wait
in a tanning pit, with skulls and coins,
for the times to change. We'll walk you
in the afterlife or dream you in the past's sweet rumour,
we'll stop suddenly in strange cities,
scratching our heads. You'll always be the street
we're about to turn into, home at last.
Ultimate Street, ancient friend,
we'll find you yet, we'll sniff you out,
it will be perfect: preternaturally bright,
irresistibly dark, and much too late . . .

The Comeback

There I was
hunched over a *canso*
in the aparthotel,

the day grey,
the year unclear
and the bed empty.

A city again,
jackhammers and cranes,
the district

repeating itself,
rising from the mud
for the umpteenth time.

My love, I began,
what have I done
to wake up again?

From the tangle
of centuries
slipped out

to begin, set down
like a native
with someone's language

in my mouth,
someone's dismal sky
to look at.

Can I really own
these hands,
these eyes darting

from building to building,
face to face,
your absence

cunningly disguised
as a street in spate,
a bridge raised to let

alien futures through?
Not mine, surely,
any of it, who have seen

so many places,
such promising verandas,
vistas of intent,

fields of lavender and corn,
ecstasies of hawthorn
and autumn birches

and pitched
over rough seas
past stacked containers

into harbour after harbour.
My love, I began,
your absence is a tax

each journey pays.
With every mile
coins fly through my fingers,

the revenues of desire
heaped on a floor.
Did that work?

What do you think?
Stacked containers,
signage,

entering the city
on a river of names . . .
Orchards, dockyards,

desert fortresses in which
only fleetingly
you appeared,

long treks in parks,
by heron-swept waters.
There's a place

I feast on
where your head
even still

turns slowly
in my direction.
You are about to speak,

your lips are moving,
then I blink
and it's somewhere else,

I'm looking
down the length
of a long room,

you swim
through a crowd
and the building

collapses: through a crack
in the pavement
we sink

to a woodland path,
impossible songs
distracting the leaves.

My love, I began,
*there must have been a time
we called our own.*

Must have been
an aeon for hands,
for tongues

fruitful and rapid,
for waking to
love's old accords.

Silence. The crane
swings round.
Yellow hats, high-viz

vests. What began
in the orchard
arrives in the street,

what began as leaf
falls as dust,
what began as song

wakes as an argument
nailed to time,
what began as voice

freezes to edict.
Was there a day
neither of us moved?

What began in wool
is undone in satin,
where silk fell

has grown a hotel.
Al-Andalus
the nape of your neck

but a Ming curl
touches your cheek.
We rise together

to walk the dawn.
The centuries, as always,
swirl through the grasses.

Early Music

Such as, why exactly are you so
stricken? Why is it that you open
your mouth and not a thing comes out?

Where do all the words go
when you need them? Are they all just
swirling around in some beautiful cavern

of their own making? I will go to my grave
on the great slide of your silence.
Tell me, what are you keeping the language for?

Your mind moves in its cold waters.
I wait for the crack, for the great
glacier slip of your heart and what speaks it.

But I don't have eternity. So gather up
your dumb flocks, love, and let them fly.

❖

Or hover, or stray at least a little,
the littlest journey from your eyes,
your mouth to mine. What do you think
the heart is? It's a muscle map, a pulsing path,
it's the shortest distance between two empires.
In case you're there, what I want now:
a flight of messengers down the stairs,
dancing through treacherous passes,
I'd like armadas, signal fires, huge
flurries of arrival and the words bawled in the street,
i.e., it's OK for empires to crumble,
it's fine for crowns to slide and edicts to unravel.
Take your big edict hands now and write
illegibly all over my body. That, that would be a start.

❖

Well, wouldn't it? It would be something.
But the day dawns, the day comes on, pulls
you to itself and . . .
                    The thing in me you don't address, who
    gets it?
Who do you talk to in your sleep?
Who is in the screen you are breakfasting with?
I am making a planet for inattention and you will travel to it
in a slow ship. Everything you missed will be there for you,
everything you didn't see, and when you've exhausted that
you can roam the galaxy of the failure to be here when it
    counted.
And impossible telescopes will be invented through which
time and again we will hunt for the miserable speck of you,
and never find it.

❖

Can't begin this or end it. I tried. I did try. I lay beside you
and looked at you, I walked the ends of the earth
or at least as far as the other room
and looked back at your immobile body.
I mean, no one expects sleep to be an act of communication
but how you lift before me, how you rise and rise
and drift out the open window and never come back,
though you're here, you open your eyes
and the world comes to you, a planet shrunk
to a slit in the blackout blind, ghost star
of the abstracted mind . . . and then I pray:
some second spirit wake in us now
to take these threads of morning up, a day
we might yet make and make till it ends up ours . . .

The Trek

So let the mountain heal
what the city can't
the car drive
past the spreading estates
our boots
find the lane again
where the sheep stare out
with such
astonished concentration
we must be saviours, messiahs
struggling to arrive

past skewed meadows
and shaking trees
the gated, murderous villas
up the steep road
unspeaking, through
the massed pines forgetful
continuously upward
to where the path
gives way to rock
and even the mind
turns granite

back to winter, where the pool
ices at the summit
and high above the sprawl
we watch our breath
flare in the cold, a pink sky edge
someone else's city
all trouble foreign
as we stand, nothing
but mountain now
white rock to white rock
settled, not looking back

Les Neiges

where has it gone
the bumblebee jumper
you wore then

the purple hat   that
jacket   what
was it   with the furred

collar   fantastic
pilot remember
how you flew then

even I forgot
lost face and footing
and floated up

oh such glad
disquiet   your
laugh   the long

dress the long
evenings   Conways
The Clarence   The Lord

Edward   Werburgh
Street   the ghosts
of fishes past

where is your grin
in the video intercom
the room

where we lay
on the infinitely shedding
blue carpet   what

was wrong with it
a live thing
an unkillable animal

growing while we slept
on the knobbly futon
still

come back all of it
even that   even
the carpet   and the pearl

fisherman trembling
as the meal is assembled
come on intercom

erupt in the hall
see   even now
the rains have gone

the snows have melted
the years open
I lift the handset

to buzz you in

Renewing the Contract

In the old house
childhood negotiates its terms,
light clatters into the hall
and the tenants shift in their flats.

Here's a hat
on a permanent lease, here's
the pattern of a dress. Blankets tumble
and stars gather above the orchard.

A door opens and closes, trees
open and close, the great wept willow
collapses and rises, you can touch
the hair of the rope of the swing and fly.

You can listen, year after year,
to shufflings and footfalls,
voices on the stair, a key in the door.
Here the joke renews its contract

and the pinprick dot of the television
warms into revelation again.
You look through a window
that has followed you everywhere

or it looks through you,
snaps every interior
and fixes you to the brickwork
like an image from Doisneau.

It's not that you return to the house:
the house invents your coming to it,
you wake to an armful of sun
like someone else's fiction.

The river climbs up to the garden
and the branches of the willow
have wrapped themselves carefully
around your vanished body.

Walking Home

This is your journey, up and down the canal like a clockwork
  soldier
counting off the bridges, hero of the dog kilometres, the
  leashed life?

Try at least: slip back, fall down, gallop layer by layer
through shifting textures, come with your sculpted insoles

where history claws the mud and curses in your ear, tumble
down the vertical park where no one is living and no one

is entirely dead; the centuries hang like apples on the trees,
unkillable wattle, unending stone, every morsel, every bone.

If there's a beginning, a first, awkward stumbling to the
  clearing,
a difficult but finally successful fording of the river, if the
  ash pit

opens, the skulls cavort, the myths crawl back from the woods,
if the suburbs slide, the tyre centres sink, the longboats
  poke through the dung,

go with it, take a leaf out of the dog's book, follow your nose,
follow the washing line past doublet and hose to where Olaf
  has hung

his shaggy jerkin, walk the seven hundred cities from here to
  there,
let the spaniel bark at pigs and horses, and when you return,
  both of you,

mud-strewn, bewildered, somehow comforted, plant your
  feet
very lightly on the towpath and take the long way home. .

Vision

Sometimes all I see is a line of down pipes and footscrapers,
a dog's eye view of the world, long red terrace and the
ghosts of uplifted feet.

Recovery

What am I getting at? Today just this,
out of the park and into the brick
where the sun strikes it, no, *leaks, fizzes,*
parties right through it from the secret heart
of Pembroke Street to where I stand
on the other side as if
after long absence embraced, invited again,
waiting to cross
into the lit place . . .

The Visited

Someone else is here now
not me
not anyone I know
someone stiff-spirited
and unfree
ghost of a girl forgotten
some child's child wandered
from the path, poor
stray foostered and fumbled
set loose in these eyes staring
beyond you
you
who do not belong to me
who come crowding into the room
with someone else's story in your arms
who is it
you look at?
Who owns these
broken bones?
A strange light slopes in from the fields
but doesn't find me
forget your flowers, forget
everything you brought
look for
the story in me
heaped and tumbled
the torn child
known once, the mist girl
missed swirl
skittering at the room's edge
take her by the hand
urge her to the centre
let the room be lit by her
and listen.

Inheritances

How much of you is me?
I face you across the narrow desk, ask
how many of your days creep into mine,
which midnights are yours, which waking
bleakness jointly owned, which dreams
repeat their restless codes.

Someone who knew us
or hunched over machines fed with the evidence
might calibrate the input, might calculate
how many thousand steps I take are yours,
which breaths, which
snags in the blood tracks, the zeptosecond
where our silences collide.

Ache I can only imagine
flies between us, settles in,
all the unguessed history, unloved hours,
long dormitory afternoons, the wreck of home,
a thousand greys, threads of an endless uniform
folding into my own years
along with words, a certain syntax,
the print of grammar like a dimple, a wrinkle,
the ways a mouth will turn or a neck incline.

Here's glumness, misery, their code secure,
but why not also
lightness, heart-lift, the instinct for more
that makes me want to imagine,
wherever you've gone,
you've inherited yourself, in full spate, somewhere
the days mingle without embarrassment,
the child inherits the child. *Inherit me*,
I want to say.

It's late here, hours we can't disguise go on turning
and I'm back there again, in midlands chill,
in your last place, the home of the unhomed
where something beyond measure stares at the wall,
wanders corridors tricked with dressers
and pretty tables,
as if the wood could call us back,
as if furniture could save us;
and something — a silence, a word, a furious

blank embrace — steals into the car
as it crawls down the avenue and speeds
helplessly towards the city.

Funeral

into the ground everything goes
the uniform, the wedding dress
bib and bride and dancing go

the chewed up pen, the classrooms go
your parents go, falling again, all the thoughts
that never touched on us

an army crosses over, short hair
long hair, skirts and dresses
skin and bone, flats and houses

the central heating boiler goes
the coalman's black face
fields go and cities go, gardens go

and garden centres, wheelbarrows go
and trellis fences, rooms and windows
go, your eyes go, combs and hairpins

your first cry goes, your last word
your husband's arms, your touches
fall with the rest on a crowded shore

The Meadow

Where is it, the poem in which
we walk across a meadow lit
by soul light, afterglow, the burn
of recognition spreading

from corner to corner,
edge to edge as we ache
towards, infinitely towards,
not quite believing our eyes,

not quite trusting the grasses,
hardly daring to breathe
the air in which we both
too late appear, one of us

raising a hand, one of us opening
the conversation in which
everything is forgiven, everything
forgotten, where is it, that one?

Through the Gate

Babylon's dust
but your blue gate
is still in the world, Ishtar.
Lions, dragons, aurochs
bare their teeth
in the cool of the Pergamon
and maybe so do you
lost goddess of love and war
empress of mayhem and tantrum.

The blue tiles dazzle us.
Outside, the monumental stretch
of Unter den Linden
and another great gate
someone might yet
delicately transport
to a promising plain
or some bright new star
with an eye for the past.

Maybe you're there already, Ishtar,
crazier than ever, observing the rites
as the armies mass
and the exiles shuffle through
shedding coats and wallets
emptying their cases in a pit.
Seven times you brush your hair
and sniff them out: wolf-man, lion, emperor;
seven garments falling to the floor
seven kinds of fury trembling at the door . . .

So Much

for Kay Hoare 1929- 2017

So much has gone already
the stone flagged kitchen shaking
with argument and laughter
the chair by the range and the dogs in attendance
the three dogs of summer
long scattered
your own patience at the heart of the drama
boots on, tending the cattle
tending us
leading us across the vanished land
continually patrolled

fields still lit and wholly occupied
mornings hurried into
as if the world might fail

whatever we did even this late
we accomplish
the yard swept
the water brought from the stream
the hay made
while the sun loiters on the desk

whatever we carried we still bear
still wakes in our hands to come with us again
the dogs by our side

and the radio sings from its dusty shelf
bringing the world
to where we crouch
rapt in the parlour
as the milk hits the angled pail

Winterreise

Schubert/Müller

winter line, the voice
thrilling its despair

a stranger I landed here
a stranger I leave now

not of my own choosing the time
but stumbling through the dark

for companion
the moon-lent shadow

the summer held us, summer
spoke for us

now hand in vanished hand
we walk the winter path

let the dogs howl at the moon
in front of her father's gate

for everything changes
let snow whiten the meadow

for everything changes

I leave you this
I write it on your gate

❖

love
the weathervane turning
on the roof of her house

and she will thrive

❖

I will converse
with the frozen earth

I will
talk the snow from the meadow

thin grass, forgotten earth
speak to me

❖

how these
images persist
incessantly repeat
so I must move like a ghost

from one to the other
and back   from the doorway
to the well from   the well
to the spreading tree

soul tree
I seemed to enter
its bark my breath its leaves
my song

I passed it in darkness
and couldn't look or listen
but knew even then
I'd feel its branches tremble

down the absent years
that I would wake
as long as I lived to see
your face, your name

shaken from the air

❖

when the ice cracks
when the grass
begins to grow
when the sun
melts the snow

let me go with it
sorrow find the river
find field and hedge
flow to where she lives
harder grip the gate

as it falls from it

❖

all that
pulsing, driving
headlong fever
of the river in spate

now locked tight
in winter's prison
river-tree I'll carve her name
on your frozen bark

I'll write the day
I saw her first, the
very time, as
long as winter lasts
this ice my witness

❖

in larksong arrived
when lindens bloomed

the town *en fête*
the streets festooned

in larksong
and linden roar

I came to you
every note encompassing

every leaf open
I came to you

walking on air, on
the song path

as now
cold as it is

I walk on fire
I walk

down the bitter street
escorted by crows

❖

here I come
in cold comfort
the frostman
white with years

but then comes
the thaw
my hair is black again
the years have melted away

and I must wander
until the cold returns
and frost can no longer
whiten my hair

❖

the watchdogs are barking
and rattling their chains
the people are dreaming
of what they can't have

drive me out, vigilant dogs
don't let me rest
when it's time for bed
devour these dreams

fallen from my head

❖

this is where I live now
winter my only news
a black gale blowing
ice hardening the grass

this ridiculous
procession of loss
where I reach for
a skein of summer

to touch
my winter mind, sunlight
to snow body, lit words
to hurdy gurdy winding

from the market's edge
its unwelcome song

yet he turns the handle
insisting, even smiling

and however the dogs bark
and the citizens yell
he holds his frozen ground
and sings

will sing me now
should I come to him

❖

winter line, the voice
soaring, descending

and yet   and yet
something beyond memory
stirs in the wind

this far in
I can't tell if I ever touched your body
if there ever was a body
or a house or a promise

the land keeps vanishing
the deer shake their antlers
like something I have almost remembered
this far wintered
what in us can believe in spring
this huddled famished forested
comprehend
the feasts of summer

the gate swings open by itself

❖

alien then
as now
of *fremde* land
in someone else's house
estranged and foreign
even to myself
wandering here and there
an other a Fremdling
in cold sun

strange I came to this shore
strange must start out again

Where Are You Going?

for Enda

Where the grass path, butter path
persist
from wrist to wrist;

where the bridle path, mountain pass
coil through us,
the rock path rears

and scrapes our fingertips;
where the cloud path, boat path
set out their stall

and the bay runs
the length of your spine;
where the harbour heaves up

and comes to stay,
waves lapping at the chair;
where the whelk path, snipe path are

and the long road long taken
wakes in us, the egret
slips under the sheet;

where the thrush path is,
the sorrel path;
where the skylark flits

above the scrub
and the orchid
descends on your eyelid;

where lizards trail and snails progress,
a storm breaks open
the ancient midden,

shells at our feet,
the old fires raked again;
where we can roam

the shark path, whale path,
where the gannets
and shearwaters dive,

where the puffins hold up time
and the dolphins repeatedly
flare in the room.

Offers

These aisles of unlikeness
a kind of perfection
as if here we might be, when it's all over,
walking through fields of Lidl finding

among the lawnmowers and beetroots
what we always half knew we half needed
but blind to the instinct and quelling desire
yet failed to achieve

and this is what carried through:
how we moved, mixing and matching
forests and plums, steamers, toys,
the mutilated flickering on a screen,

dawdling through it all, filling our arms
with what we found,
unlikeness our element, our prayers
the trundling of trolleys in the aisles.

At Staigue Fort

The sign on the gate
asks for a coin to compensate
our trespass. Maybe he's right,
whoever owns it, maybe the place
is absolutely his, the millennia

sing in his blood, he wakes
to ghost cattle lowing
from deep inside the fort.
Something's here, some long
possession holds the stones

and climbs the steps
to walk the walls and peer
from mountain to sea and back.
Is there a ship, a hawk?
Has a dragonfly

somehow landed on a blade of grass,
a stag's breath slipped in
to haunt the valley? The watched sun
goes down, the dark
creeps to the fort

setting off horns, alarms,
finds us lying
weightless in the ring's dead centre.
Something's here
in the shadows drawing

across the stones'
giant press, the trespass
our bodies lightening the grass,
lifted from it, held as if
by a thousand fingertips . . .

Reach

It's in the stones
lapped by the falling stream
in the mud that follows
the steep climb to the gate
and the grass that comes after

in the broken hut
where the sheep dawdle
the wind on the stones
the sea stretched behind us
and the hidden village

it's in our steps
light and heavy, sunk and lifted
in the delicate
passages, ascending, descending
opening, closing

it's there
the coves in the spread bay
the trail coiling in
to the heart of the mountain
it's in the gaps, the heather

a chough dances up
and flies to his rock
it's in stonechat in raven
your back as I stand behind you
where you sit like a queen

like a queen with
the landscape in your lap
the fields sweeping down
to the bay's long finger
grass and stone and sea

and it's how we do this
year after year
as if it all belonged to us
and whatever we did we'd always be
moving through land, blessed by the reach

of a long path

After Borges

I TO A MINOR POET

Where are the days you spent on earth,
all the joy and anguish
that were your universe?

The river of years has washed them away;
now you survive
as an entry in the index.

Proudly they gather, the gods' gifts, immortal.
Of you, dark friend, all we know
is that one evening you heard the nightingale.

Walking fields of asphodels, your slighted shade
must think the gods harsh
but the days are a tangle of paltry needs

and is there really a blessing richer
than the ash of which oblivion's made?
For others the gods kindled

a persistent light: see
how it shines in every crevice, finds every flaw
and in the end shrivels the rose it treasures.

They were kinder to you, brother, passing you by,
leaving you to the nightingale in the garden
in the thrill of a dusk which will never darken.

2 TO THE SON

It wasn't I who fathered you, it was the dead:
my father, his father, their fathers before them
tracing their way through a maze of loves
all the way from Adam, from the deserts
of Cain and Abel, a dawn so distant
mythology blocks the view. And here
they are now: flesh and bone, their feet
in the future, their breath on your shoulder.
They crowd around, I can feel them press,
we, you, those yet to come, the sons
you'll conceive, the latest of the line,
the red line of Adam, and I am
all the others too, eternity hurrying
in the bones of time . . .

3 TO A SAXON POET

The snows of Northumbria have felt
and forgotten the print of your feet
and the nights are uncountable that lie
between us, my ghostly brother.
Slow in the slow dark you'd work
your metaphors of swords on the seas,
the horror in the pine woods
and the loneliness the days brought.
Where should we look for your face
and your name? In the halls of oblivion.
I'll never know how life was for you
when you were a man on the earth,
you who followed the hard paths of exile
and now live only in iron verses.

4 A COMPASS

Everything comes down to a word in a language
someone or something, night and day,
is writing in an infinite confusion.
This is the history of the world, Carthage

and Rome, you, me, everyone, my life
which is beyond me, its torment
of chance, mystery and secret codes
and all of Babel's discords.

Behind the name the nameless lies,
today I felt its shadow settle
in the clear blue compass needle

stretching to the limit of the seas,
like a clock seen in a dream
or a bird suddenly moving in its sleep.

Lost Properties

How often have I sat on the edge
of the pouring fountain looking back

at the house assembling itself brick by dusty brick
the glass floating into the waiting frames

walked floors grazed by the hems of delicate dresses
by my own breath and my ears pressed to the wood

to catch the footsteps of everyone who isn't there . . .
Over and over

branches cavort   a street gathers pace   coffee drifts up
and whatever I am
pulls on its coat and leaves the room

Possession

Ten thousand steps, the city at my feet
the city *in* my feet
ten thousand steps in sun and rain
park and street
each one the soul
of a nineteenth-century flâneur

ten thousand poets marching in step
along the canal, across Baggot Street bridge
and up Pembroke Road
ten thousand Patrick Kavanaghs
on eternal patrol

if steps were stakes or nails
or beads playing
in the lock's
reliable roar
then this
solider possession would make the place
ten thousand times my own

but the brutal pedometer
has nothing on its mind
every midnight the city returns
as through a blank and lonely gate
and like Cinderella sits home alone
the flailing prince finds no one left to kiss
and ten thousand steps shrink to none

Lived Here

Behind this brick
this glass
in this house
for twelve years
for six months
a week
an instant
incomparable

how the light fell
in just the right way
the fire blazed miracles
and the conversation
after the work was done
fizzed and glittered

here
right here
here flourished
here angels
partied
here cushions flew

in this house
marvellously
if all too briefly
here fulfilled
stretched
here loosed
and tumbled

or not

or sat
gruff-mouthed

and thin-spirited
in the draught
the heart unlit
staring in
staring out
through the glass

here
we do not know
who you are

here the unremembered
the unconsoled
the lost crowd
staring
through the glass

the print
of their breath
the press
of their lives

such fierce
endurance

through the glass
above which
even as we speak
someone else's tenancy
is hammered to the brick

Nudge

And then I'll walk
up the deviceless avenue
notified by trees, alerted
by fuchsia, montbretia;

I'll step
over the stream
touched by dragonflies,
woken by reeds;

I'll be a drudge, a bore
in the industry of the air,
press my face against the grass
till it lets me in.

The sky will remind me,
the mountains recognize me,
the clouds
will measure my breaths

and when I've fallen
over the edge
the tasks will unattach
and snore beside me

till I wake
to warbler, corncrake,
head in the sedge, never
so delicately nudged.

Older

Could this be you
turning up again
suddenly surefooted
wanting the news
me coming on
more brother than son
older than you ever were
yet still unsure
showing off the neighbourhood
telling you, if I dared,
how I wore your sweater for years
told time by your watch
until it disappeared

Could this be us
patrolling the streets
my anxious steps
persuading you home
Here's my daughter you never knew
she shines in her bones like the sun
here's my wife with a hug to greet you
banished the days
in which everything and nothing
repeatedly occurred
where you wandered
absent of light, absent of hurt

And this be the parting
your teasing question
How much more do you know
who are so far ahead?
Not a thing but to love the steps
wish I could follow
not lead, there was something
I might offer yet

a sweater against the chill
or that I might stop, reach into a pocket
and pull out the miraculous watch
still going, still full of time
and you'd stretch out your hand
as I slipped it on and fell behind

Poem in August

Uniform, bag, accoutrements, the restive phone's
sweet urgencies. The floor that holds us

doesn't: the boards span aeons, my feet
locked, roots of a tree long grown. Talk

to the forest, your eyes say, your deer's feet running
in their own time, this tree's busy, this tree's *gone*.

Kleist's Grave

So this is the place.
Here by the lake
I stumble on the path,
the last journey
marked by signs,
the coloured numbers
of an acoustic trail
and all of this
civic greenery
before the railed grave
on its little mound
hardly a step from the inn
where everyone agreed
you were both
the picture of content.
Everything here
as controlled and orderly
as your own
final orderliness:
coffee, a stroll,
last letters . . .
Yet you could hardly
have been less at home.
The world is strange, you said,
as you flitted
pell-mell through it.
The world is always
the other side
of a half-open door
through which, disbelievingly,
we stare.
You sang and suffered
like someone
the age itself had conjured,
its gift to you,

your one true possession
and surest lodging,
this path
laid down in the bone
to await its time.

Haus der Wannsee-Konferenz

Opened on 20 January 1992, on the fiftieth anniversary of the conference where the Final Solution was determined.

How much can a place know?
Not much, or the gravelled entrance, you'd think,
would have taken off, the roses flown, the cobbled path
forgone the mansion
for an alternative destination.
Nothing here could have stood
but would have crumpled and slid, somehow,
into the toy lake.
Wouldn't it?
But it all just shines; the end of the world
will have these trees and villas,
these sailboats dawdling from shore to shore,
this builder's labourer moving
unhurriedly down the street.
The typewriters, you'd think, the very paper . . .
but the apparatus didn't rupture,
the flashbulbs self-destruct
and the language is still here, in its glass.
Eternal numbers, arguments, protocols.
Someone shouts for coffee. The bricks
hold firm. You'd think . . .
but everything's still here, everything's waiting.
Somewhere
light pours through the windows
of a room like this,
someone opens
the redacted conversation.
The bricks hold firm.

Bruegel: The Wedding in the Barn

The leering, brutal figures
squat in their island habitat,
the gypsies caught on camera
throw a punch, adjust a dress

and at the wedding in the barn
the peasants grope and tumble,
twist and flail. Have you seen
this one? The thin-faced relatives

squabble over a purse of coins,
the sharp-nosed others take it all in,
the pipers check each other out,
it's a race, the notes on fire. *What*

would you do if the kettle
boiled over? This one's had it,
his head slumped on the table,
hell is a furious music. *What*

would I do only fill it again.
The short one in the reality house
is evil, Cheyenne is
the bubbly one, her tiara's

askew. The fat
peasant lunges at the cameraman.
Bruegel sighs: the ratings are up
but the complaints are pending.

Fake tan, oiled muscles, that old
hunger for the authentic, the white
headdresses, the faces
outliving effort, shot

after shot to be trawled through.
Who cares that the budget's blown
if we have art enough to nail the tune?
Smile, or not. You'll always have the barn.

The Conversation

for Martin Hayes and David Power

Even here
in the pink-chaired conference-cum-function room
with its frills and fusses
even here the carpet perks up
the cream pillars cock their ears
before the reels are loosed
the notes explode, the parts repeat
fiddler leaning to piper leaning over

and now both have left
for the place
where the music goes beyond their playing of it
ghost bride and ghost groom
leap through the room, melt
and brighten again
'You lead, I'll follow.' And they go
where they haven't exactly gone before

and won't exactly go again.
The bow waits
and plunges, the pipes pick up the thread
and as for us, smiling hard, it's as if
we'd taught ourselves to talk like this
somehow flown
to where bow and chanter utter
the very heart of the conversation

The Gravity Wave

Where next for this gust
printing itself on your dress,
catching the rim of your hat, riffing
in the strands of your hair?

Maybe the same place
as this single breath, this turning
of neck towards neck,
this widening of the eyes and whatever

loosens behind,
soul-stretch, spirit-drift
that have left us and gone
pouring down the billennia,

rippling, thinning,
fainter by the second but lodged forever,
infinitesimally measurable
where two particles conversing

almost falter, almost alter
as they register
the micron's micron, the hair's breadth's whisper
of what passed between us.

Acknowledgements

Acknowledgements are due to the editors of the following publications where some of these poems, or versions of them, were published or broadcast first: *The Irish Times, Lines of Vision, Irish Writers on Art* (edited by Janet McLean, National Gallery of Ireland, 2014), *Metamorphic: 21st Century Poets Respond to Ovid* (edited by Nessa O'Mahony and Paul Munden, Recent Work Press, 2017), *The Past Is A Foreign Country* (Anita Groener exhibition catalogue, 2018, Limerick City Gallery of Art), *Poetry Ireland Review* and RTÉ Radio.

Thanks are due to Literature Ireland for a residency in Berlin in 2016.